SILVER

A TRUE BOOK®
by
Salvatore Tocci

Children's Press®
A Division of Scholastic Inc.

New York Toronto London Auckland Sydney
Mexico City New Delhi Hong Kong
Danbury, Connecticut

This Navajo belt is made of silver.

Reading Consultant
Julia McKenzie Munemo, EdM
New York, New York

Content Consultant
John A. Benner
Austin, Texas

The photo on the cover shows a variety of silver products. The photo on the title page shows bars of silver.

The author and the publisher are not responsible for injuries or accidents that occur during or from any experiments. Experiments should be conducted in the presence of or with the help of an adult. Any instructions of the experiments that require the use of sharp, hot, or other unsafe items should be conducted by or with the help of an adult.

Library of Congress Cataloging-in-Publication Data

Tocci, Salvatore.
Silver / by Salvatore Tocci.
    p. cm. — (A true book)
    Includes bibliographical references and index.
    ISBN 0-516-23696-2 (lib. bdg.)   0-516-25572-X (pbk.)
    1. Silver—Juvenile literature. I. Title. II. Series.
TN761.6.T63 2005   3205 8645 2/05
546'.654—dc22
                                                    2004013145

CHILDREN'S PRESS, and A TRUE BOOK™, and associated logos are trademarks and or registered trademarks of Scholastic Library Publishing. SCHOLASTIC and associated logos are trademarks and or registered trademarks of Scholastic Inc.
1 2 3 4 5 6 7 8 9 10 R 14 13 12 11 10 09 08 07 06 05

Contents

You can see in these windows, but if the people in those apartments looked out, it would be like looking at a one-way mirror.

What Do You See Out the Window?

Have you ever looked out a window at night from inside a room that was well lit? If you have, all you might have seen was an image of your face on the glass. If there were people outside, they would have been able to see you. However, you probably could not see them. This is similar to the way a one-way mirror works.

The police sometimes watch through a one-way mirror as a suspect is being questioned in another room. However, the suspect cannot see the police. How does a one-way mirror work? The answer has to do with the way the mirror is made.

An ordinary mirror is made by covering a piece of glass with a thin layer of silver. You see yourself in the mirror because the silver reflects, or bounces back, any light that strikes it. As a result, you see your face and anything else that is reflected by the silver.

A one-way mirror is made by applying the thin layer of silver so that it does not cover the entire glass.

Instead, it is applied in vertical stripes that are separated by narrow gaps. If you look at the silver stripes, you see a reflection. However, if you look through a gap, you can see to the other side.

So, why can the police, but not the suspect, see through these gaps? The suspect is always in a room that is well lit. The bright light reflects off the silver stripes in the one-way mirror, preventing the suspect from seeing through the gaps. On the other hand, the police are always in a room that is very dark. They can see through the gaps because the silver stripes do not reflect much of anything in the dark. As you will learn in this book, silver is used for more than just making one-way mirrors.

What Is Silver?

Silver is an element. An **element** is the building block of matter. **Matter** is the stuff or material that makes up everything in the universe. This book, the chair you are sitting on, and even you are made of matter.

There are millions of different kinds of matter. However, there are just a few more than one hundred different elements. How can so many different kinds of matter be made up of so few elements? Think about the English language. Just twenty-six letters can be arranged to make up all the words in the English language. Likewise, the one hundred or so elements can be arranged to make up all the kinds of matter in the universe.

Every element has a name and a symbol made up of one, two, or three letters. The symbol for silver is Ag. This symbol comes from *argentum*, the Latin word for silver. The early Romans, however, were not the first people to admire silver. Some six thousand years ago, the ancient Egyptians wore jewelry made of silver.

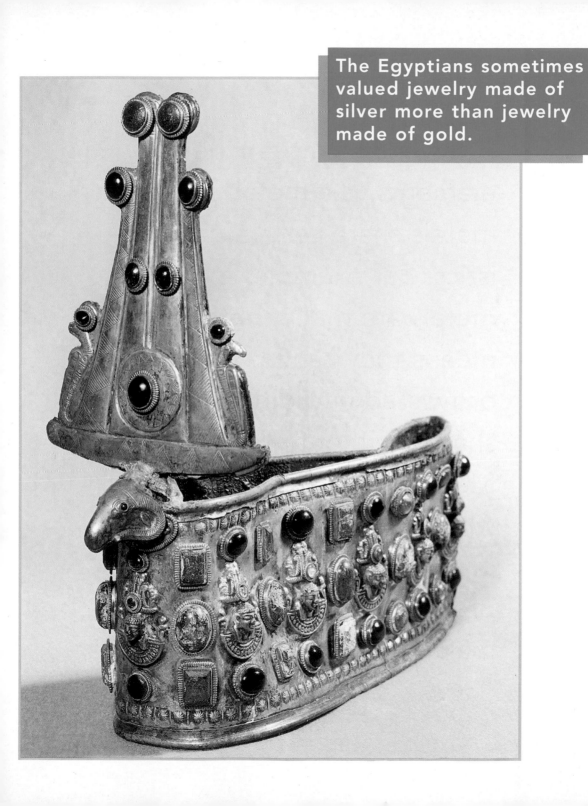

The Egyptians sometimes valued jewelry made of silver more than jewelry made of gold.

Silver, like most other elements, is a metal. Many metals share certain characteristics. For example, many metals are **malleable**, which means they can be hammered or twisted into different shapes without breaking. Many metals are also **ductile**, which means they can be drawn into a thin wire or pressed thin. Silver is both malleable and ductile.

The one characteristic that makes metals stand apart from all the other elements is their ability to allow electricity to pass through them. In fact, of all the elements, silver is the best **conductor** of electricity.

Silver is a bright, shiny, grayish metal. Unlike some metals, silver does not corrode, or rust. Silver, however, does tarnish easily. Tarnish usually appears as a black coating on silver. This coating is formed when silver reacts, or combines, with another element called sulfur. The sulfur can come from the air, foods, or even your hands. Silver and sulfur combine to form tarnish, which is a **compound**. A compound is a substance that is made when two or more different elements, such as silver and sulfur, join together.

The tarnish that forms on silver is a compound called silver sulfide.

Removing the Tarnish

Learn how you can remove the tarnish from silver without polishing it. Get a pan that is deep enough to hold a tarnished piece of silver. Line the bottom of the pan with aluminum foil. Place the silver object on the foil. Sprinkle about 1 cup of baking soda over the foil.

Ask an adult to help you boil some water in a pot. Pour the hot water into the pan. The tarnish should begin to vanish. What happens to the foil?

Why Is Silver a Precious Metal?

Silver, like gold, is a precious metal. Precious metals are valuable because they are in great demand, but their supply is very limited. Nearly seventy elements are more common than silver. Most of the world's supply of silver comes from **ores**. An ore is a substance found in nature that contains a valuable element or compound. Ores are found in Earth's crust. On dry land, the crust can extend up to 30 miles (50 kilometers) below the surface. Mines have to be dug to reach the ores buried in the crust.

Nearly 75 percent of silver comes from ores that are actually mined for other metals. For example, galena is an ore that is mined for the iron it contains. However, galena also contains a very small amount of silver that is recovered along with the iron. About 25 percent of silver comes from ores that are specifically mined for their silver content. The main ore that is mined for its silver is called argentite.

In the late 1850s, miners discovered a huge supply of argentite in Nevada. This mine became known as the Comstock Lode. So much silver was recovered that the huge supply caused its price to fall. At the time, the U.S. government was using silver to make coins, including silver dollars. As the price of silver continued to fall, the miners in Nevada began to worry that the government would no longer mint silver coins and that they would be out of a job.

Nevada became a state in 1864. Shortly afterward, its two senators pushed through a law that required the government to make millions of silver dollars every month. This demand kept the Comstock Lode in business. A small mint was even opened in Carson City, Nevada. The supply of silver from the Comstock Lode eventually ran out. Soon after, the Carson City mint was closed.

THE
COMSTOCK LODE
DISCOVERED 8 JUNE 1859

AT HEAD OF SIX MILE CANYON
WASHOE MINING DISTRICT
VIRGINIA CITY, NEVADA

THIS MONUMENT OF ORE FROM
EVERY NEVADA COUNTY
COMMEMORATES THE ONE-
HUNDREDTH ANNIVERSARY OF
THE DISCOVERY OF SILVER.

This monument marks the site where silver was discovered at the Comstock Lode.

Most of the coins that were minted in Carson City were eventually melted down so that the silver could be used by the military during World War I. The silver dollars that survived are now worth much more than their face value.

The United States was not the first to use silver to make coins. The first silver coins were made about 2,600 years ago by people living in an

This silver dollar was minted in Carson City, Nevada, in the 1880s. Today, it is worth several hundred dollars.

area that is now part of Turkey. From there, the practice of using silver to make coins quickly spread to other parts of the world, including Greece and Rome. In ancient times, one of the main uses of silver was in making coins. Today, only about 5 percent of the silver that is mined is used to make coins. The remaining 95 percent of the silver has other uses.

How Else Is Silver Used?

Today, silver's main use is in photography. Both photographic film and paper contain a silver compound. When it is struck by light, the silver in this compound turns into pure silver and becomes darker. The silver helps to form the images that appear

29

Silver is also used to produce the images on X-rays.

on black-and-white film or paper. Color prints are also made with the use of silver, along with dyes that are added.

The second most common use of silver today is in making jewelry. The use of silver to make jewelry has a long history. The ancient Egyptians made silver jewelry 2,500 years ago. However, there is one problem with using silver to make jewelry. Although it is harder than gold, pure silver is still rather soft and can bend.

To prevent the jewelry from bending or breaking, the silver is first mixed with another metal to produce an **alloy**. An alloy is different from a compound. In a compound, the elements are joined together. In an alloy, the elements are mixed together, but they retain their individual properties.

Shining Like Silver

Learn how light can make something look silver. Ask an adult to light a candle. Use pliers to hold a penny in the flame. The penny should turn black. The burning wax produces an element called carbon. Carbon is black and collects on the penny. Cover both sides of the penny with a thick layer of carbon. Then place it in a glass of water. Look at the penny through the side of the glass. The black carbon should look like bright silver. Tiny air bubbles are trapped between the carbon layer and the penny. When you look from the side, the light strikes these air bubbles, and they appear silver. What color do you see if you look down from the top of the glass?

The alloy used to make jewelry is made by mixing silver with either lead or copper. These elements make the alloy harder and tougher than pure silver. The most common silver alloy is known as sterling silver.

Although it is an alloy, sterling silver still tarnishes. The black tarnish that forms on sterling silver jewelry can rub off on the skin or on clothing. In addition, any

These items are made of sterling silver, which is 92.5 percent silver and 7.5 percent copper.

copper that is added to the alloy may turn green. This black or green tarnish may also rub off on skin or clothing. Therefore, sterling silver jewelry needs to be cleaned frequently. In addition to jewelry, sterling silver is also used to make eating utensils, serving trays, and decorative objects.

Silver's properties make it useful in other ways. Because it is an excellent conductor of electricity, silver is used in electrical switches. Almost all electrical appliances, including telephones, dishwashers, microwaves, and televisions, use silver switches.

Silver is also an excellent conductor of heat. This property makes it valuable for use in rear-window defrosters in cars. The horizontal lines you see running across the rear window are made from a ceramic compound that contains silver. This compound is baked onto the window at very high temperatures. The heat that passes through the silver in the ceramic compound warms the window to about 85 degrees Fahrenheit (30 degrees Celsius).

Silver is also used in medicine. In fact, the use of silver as a medicine dates back to the ancient Egyptians. They used silver vessels whenever they had to store water and other liquids for a long period of time to keep the liquids from spoiling. What the Egyptians did not know is that silver kills the bacteria, or germs, that would otherwise spoil the water. Pioneers traveling in wagon trains across the United States used silver coins to keep the water and milk stored in wooden casks from spoiling. Today, silver is used in water filters

Farmers in the Australian outback still suspend silverware in tanks such as this one to prevent the water stored inside from spoiling.

for purifying swimming pool and drinking water.

A substance known as colloidal silver is still used to treat infections. The silver works because of its ability to absorb oxygen. Without oxygen, the germs that cause the infection die. Before antibiotics were first used in the 1940s, about four dozen different silver compounds were used to treat infections and various diseases.

Fun Facts About Silver

- About 1 billion tons of ore have to be mined to get about 70 pounds (32 kg) of silver.

- Only 1 ounce of silver is needed to make about five thousand color photographs.

- People who have silver in the fillings in their teeth will feel a shock when they bite on a piece of aluminum foil.

- A washing machine has about fifteen electrical parts made of silver.

- The U.S. Mint stopped using silver to make coins in 1967.

- An object made of nickel silver actually contains no silver at all. Rather, nickel silver is an alloy made of nickel, copper, and zinc.

- To find out if something is silver, test it with a magnet. If the object is attracted to the magnet, it is not silver.

- A compound called silver iodide can be scattered on clouds by planes in an effort to produce rain during a drought.

To Find Out More

If you would like to learn more about silver, check out these additional resources.

Books

Llewellyn, Claire. **Metal.** Franklin Watts, 2002.

Watt, Susan. **Silver.** Benchmark Books, 2002.

Organizations and Online Sites

The Silver Institute
http://www.silverinstitute.org

Read more about how silver is used for various purposes by clicking on any of the links under "Silver Uses."

Use of Silver for Treating Diseases
http://www.mts.net/ ~revive/uses.txt

This is a list of the more than one hundred diseases and medical conditions, such as warts, flu, and pneumonia, that have been treated with silver.

The United States Mint
http://www.usmint.gov/ about_the_mint/mint _history/index.cfm?action =silver_dollar_1700s

This site provides information about the history of the silver dollar during the 1700s, 1800s, and 1900s.

Silver— The Precious Metal
http://www.desertusa.com/ mag99/aug/papr/silver.html

Learn more about the mining of silver, including the best-known ancient mines located in Greece. This site also provides more information about silver's properties, such as its melting and boiling points.

Important Words

alloy substance made by mixing a metal with one or more other elements

compound substance formed when two or more elements are joined

conductor substance through which electricity or heat passes

ductile capable of being drawn into a wire or pressed thin

element building block of matter

malleable capable of being hammered or twisted into different shapes without breaking

matter stuff or material that makes up everything in the universe

ore material found in nature from which a valuable substance, such as iron, can be extracted

Index

Meet the Author

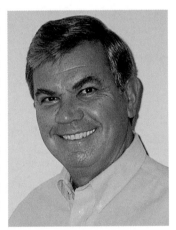

Salvatore Tocci is a science writer who lives in East Hampton, New York, with his wife Patti. He was a high school biology and chemistry teacher for almost thirty years. His books include a high school chemistry textbook and an elementary school series that encourages students to perform experiments to learn about science. He depends on silver compounds to develop black-and-white film and prints in his darkroom.

Photographs © 2005: Art Resource, NY/Bridgeman-Giraudon/Egyptian Museum, Cairo, Egypt: 13; Corbis Images: 40 (Morton Beebe), 25 (Dave G. Houser), 4 (Ted Mahieu), 30 (Ariel Skelley); PhotoEdit/Michael Newman: 17; Superstock, Inc.: 35 (Peter Harholdt), 2 (Lowe Art Museum), cover, 1; www.collectsource.com: 27 bottom, 27 center, 27 top.